Clive Grinnell.

ETERNAL SPAIN

ETERNAL SPAIN

The Spanish Rural Landscape

Photographs by Robert Frerck

Introduction by Alastair Reid

HARRY N. ABRAMS, INC., PUBLISHERS, NEW YORK

Editor: Robert Morton
Designer: Liz Trovato

Library of Congress Cataloging-in-Publication Data

Frerck, Robert.
    Eternal Spain/photographs by Robert Frerck; introduction by
Alastair Reid.
        p.   cm.
    ISBN 0-8109-3252-0 (cloth)
    1. Spain — Description and travel — 1981- — Views. 2. Spain —
Description and travel — 1981- I. Reid, Alastair 1926–
II. Title.
DP43.2.F74   1991
946.083'022'2 — dc20

                                                        91-8080
                                                        CIP

Published in 1991 by Harry N. Abrams, Incorporated, New York
A Times Mirror Company

Printed and bound in Belgium

Opposite: The skyline of Segovia, with the Guadarrama Mountains in the background.

Previous page: The hilltop village of Montefrío in Andalusia.

CONTENTS

On a narrow ridge above the plains of Castile–La Mancha, southeast of Toledo, stands a ruined castle and the windmills of Consuegra.

Sandstone cliffs called the *Mallos de Riglos* (The Ninepins) rise above the town of Riglos, northwest of Huesca, in Aragon.

Watered by the Navia River and the heavy rainfall of the Cantabrian cordillera, this fertile valley lies on the border of Galicia and Asturias, close to Spain's north coast.

A steep-walled mesa rising above the Rio Arazas dominates Ordesa National Park in the Pyrenees near the French border.

Near the headwaters of the Rio Cuervo in the Sierra de Cuenca, a waterfall spills its bounty toward the central plain.

The plains of Castile, breadbasket of the nation, roll west of Salamanca in Castile–Leon.

Poplars line the flooded shore of Lake Barasona, near Graus, east of Huesca, in Aragon.

Young vines form a pattern of green across the blackened volcanic landscape of the La Geria valley on Lanzarote in the Canary Islands.

Cork trees and wildflowers spread westward toward the Sierra de Gredos in Castile–Leon.

The jagged silhouette of Montserrat rises in the mist behind this small church in Catalonia, west of Barcelona.

The Spanish Land

A Study in Contrasts by Alastair Reid

If I were to think of a single image for what drew me to Spain and the people of Spain, it would be one of coming into a valley in the mountains, seeing a single man working in a field, stopping for one of those quintessential Spanish conversations, and feeling that here was someone sure in his skin, dignified, courteous, but direct and unapologetic, who had no doubt who he was. A wave of the arm away was his *pueblo* — his village, his family, his neighbors. Around him were his crops, his livelihood. The

GALICIA

Santiago •
• Lugo
El Grove •

ASTURIAS
Navia •
Covadonga •
Mogrevejo •
CANTABRIA

BASQUE
COUNTRY
Pamplona •
NAVARRE
Ujué •
LA RIOJA

Ordesa •
• Castillo de Loarre
• Huesca

Valle de Arán •
• Aigüe Tortes
• Pervis
CATALONIA
Tossa •
Montserrat •
Barcelona •
Tarragona •

Leon •

CASTILE-LEON

Soria •

Gormaz •

ARAGON

Turégano •
Salamanca •
Segovia •
Molina de Aragón •

Linares •
• Albarracín
• Teruel

Ávila •
MADRID ★
• Guadalajara
Rio Cuervo •

La Alberca •
Chinchón •
• Cuenca

Toledo •
VALENCIA
La Albufera •

Consuegra •

Guadalupe •
Trujillo •

CASTILE-LA MANCHA

Villajoyosa •
Alicante •

ESTREMADURA

BALEARIC
ISLANDS

MURCIA

ANDALUSIA

• Cazorla

Almodóvar del Rio •
• Córdoba

Guadix •
• La Calahorra
Tabernas •
Montefrío •
Granada •
Almería •
Seville •

Huelva •
Zahara •
• Olvera
Málaga •
El Rocío •
• Ronda
Arcos •
Jerez •
Casares •
Cádiz •

CANARY ISLANDS

terrain his arm encircled was his universe, and his place and function in it were clear to him. To it he owed his whole allegiance. The world outside his valley was of lesser importance. The equilibrium he maintained with the land in this private landscape was one that had been achieved over centuries, that had been handed on to him, and that would go on after him, given good and bad years, eternally.

There is a sense in which all Spanish villages resemble one another, although no two are alike. What they share is a human scale. They are small enough for every inhabitant to have a name, a place, and a persona in the eyes of all the others. There are no anonymous clumps of people, and no one can remain a stranger. Village societies are mainly self-governing. Work is dictated by the crop, by the climate, by the changing seasons. A bus will make its way once a day to a nearby town and back, bringing supplies, urgencies, messages, mail. The village will have ups and downs, like changes in the weather; but it will weather on.

Spaniards still identify themselves first by naming their *pueblo*, where they are from. First allegiance is to *pueblo* and family, above country and government. With this local allegiance, Spaniards have kept alive a way of life that was common in classical times and in the Middle Ages, a way of life that looks both ancient and eternal, and that gives rise to those very qualities so marked in the inhabitants of rural Spain — their independence of character, their directness, their social grace, their sense of who they are. They are on their own ground. They know where their loyalties lie. Each Spanish village, with its surrounding landscape, was a *patria chica*, a self-contained world, and at one time Spain itself was no more than an accumulation of thousands of such miniature countries. The towns and cities belonged to another, more abstract Spain. Much of Spain's history has been one of a struggle between central government and those separate local autonomies, which bred natural anarchists. It used to be said that country people all over Spain, every night before going to bed, would shake their fists in the direction of Madrid — that artificial capital decreed by Philip II in the

Olvera, one of the countless *pueblos blancos* of Andalusia, lies atop a hill crowned with the twin spires of its cathedral and the outline of a Moorish castle.

Previous page: Some of the narrowest streets in Spain may be found in the mountain village of Cazorla, in the Sierra de Cazorla, northeast of Granada.

Deserted except for a shepherd's flock, Turégano castle rises from the plains of Castile, northwest of Segovia.

middle of the great plateau of Castile, the absent monster that must be fed and supplied from all over the regions, at the center of a vast spiderweb of authority.

Spain is extraordinary in having so many of these small universes, so varying in nature, but so alike in spirit. Off the beaten track, they have remained much as they were, self-sufficient, wary of the outside world. In these rural landscapes, life had been reduced to its simplest terms by necessity. Poverty hovered always close, the climate was cruel in its extremes, and the fertility of the land depended on an unending round of hard work. Yet life was shouldered as a fate or a destiny and lived with great dignity and humanity. It did not question itself, and it had an air of deep finality about it, an air of being outside time.

You can tell Spain's main regions off on your fingers — the long strip of lush greenness along the northern Atlantic Coast, well forested and orcharded, well watered, with cattle and sheep; the immense expanse of the central Meseta, the great plains of Old and New Castile, brilliant with wheat in the growing season, but burnt bare in summer, stretching as far as the vineyards and windmills of La Mancha, where cattle have given way to sheep; and the Mediterranean coast-lines and Andalusia, where the pace is slower, the summer fiercer, the villages whiter, where the gray rock rises are dotted with green rows of olive and almond, the valleys fill with vines and fruit, and where, from beaches and small harbors, the fishing is bountiful. There are other, smaller regions — the high beauties of Aragon, descending from the dry Pyrenees through bare, pine-topped spaces to a green plain; the Balearic Islands, still pristine in their interiors, but bearing a top-heavy weight of tourist despoilment around their coastlines; the forlorn plateaus of Estremadura, sheep and cork trees, huddled villages, where many remains of Roman Spain still stand; the deserts of Almeria, trudged across by the crews of many movies, the land ultimately bone dry and unbearing; the great river courses of the Ebro and the Guadalquivir; the extraordinary salt marshes,

Las Marismas, to the south of Seville, where migrant birds shelter in winter; and the Canary Islands, volcanic eruptions that have been made fertile with a semitropical vegetation.

The enormous variety in Spanish rural landscapes makes it easy to think of them as miniature countries, separate solitudes. To enter Spain through the Pyrenees, leaving behind the heady green fuse of the French countryside, is to come upon Aragon, a landscape brown and rocky-bare, except for the green clumps close to a water source, spreading into a vast, dry, dusty expanse, broken by massive, solitary, ochre-colored cliffs, crumbled by erosion into the rounded shapes of monoliths. The view on all sides looks forlorn, planetary, unpeopled; then, round a corner, on a rise, a mountain stream is falling into a broad waterfall and, close to it, a village has taken root under a protecting brow, rimmed with the green of its carefully tended terraces, shaded by poplars, looking up to clumps of pine and fir just below the tree line. Contrasts everywhere. It seems that for every particular landscape in Spain you could find its opposite somewhere else in the country. In the fierce heat of high summer, the great plain of Castile sheds its spring green and gives way to a universal dusty dryness, and, horizon to horizon, waves of farmland, fields of sunflowers, parched earth under a huge expanse of unwavering blue sky, the earth-colored villages looking like mirages in the heat; at the same time, in the little enclosed valleys of Galicia and the Basque Country, inland from the sea, with their luminous greenness, their orchards and sheep, their great stands of chestnut trees and their lines of white poplar, water is everywhere, with a whisper of rain

On the island of Minorca in the Balearic Islands stands one of many stone monuments of the Bronze Age, believed to have been built by peoples of the eastern Mediterranean and more numerous on Minorca than anywhere else. Their purpose, like those of the megaliths of France and the British Isles, remains largely unknown, although they surely served a religious function. Some of the largest constructions, resembling huge stone igloos, were probably burial chambers.

on the wind, streams rushing to the Atlantic, drought unheard of. Water is the key. In the long, hot summers in the South, even its sound is luxurious to the ear, the splash of a bucket in a well, the trickle of a stream that was a torrent in winter. Throughout Andalusia, wherever water is, in streams and irrigation ditches, the puffs of green surrounding it stand out like oases against the red earth.

Well into this century, Spain could have been infinitely subdivided into its thousand upon thousand of smaller universes, its village outposts of rural survival. But so abruptly has Spanish society changed that present day Spain has three distinct regions: its cities and provincial towns, with their concomitant airports, factories, sports stadia, media, and new population, bent on becoming one as quickly as possible with the New Europe; its tourist retreats, strung along its Mediterranean coastline and maintained as a kind of no-man's-land, a source of revenue, like a latter-day crop; and the myriad rural landscapes, left behind in time, where people live on a level of comfort well below the cities. The Spain that opened its frontiers to Europe in 1947, after being cut off, first by its own Civil War, and then the Second World War, was a poor and backward agricultural country, threadbare and dispirited. That it has transformed itself into a responsible democracy, an active partner in the European community, highly industrialized, with more than half of its population living in cities and large towns means that Spanish society has gone through centuries of change compressed into decades, changes at which the people of rural Spain have been, as always, bystanders. The drift from the villages to the cities has been steady and eroding. Inevitably, the population of rural Spain is dwindling.

The Spanish landscape has been the setting and theater for tumultuous historical happenings, and the vestiges of that history are present on all sides, and intrude themselves into the present, the layered evidence of an immemorial past. Yet paradoxically, it may be the long shadow of that past that so sharpens the awareness of the present moment, for in Spain you immediately feel the intense presentness that Spaniards have, as though, sitting down to eat or talk,

The green fields that surround Santillana sustain numerous dairy farms.

South of Pamplona, the village of Ujué is capped by its 14th-century, fortified Gothic church and surrounded by terraced fields.

they switch off time, and immerse themselves in the occasion for as long as it lasts.

It is impossible to ignore the history of Spain, for it is tangibly present at every turn. In Menorca the *talayots*, those great clumps of stone that still stand from the Bronze Age, are surrounded by growing crops. They are as much part of the encrusted human landscape as are the Altamira caves, the Roman aquaducts, the exquisite purity of the Alhambra, and the great medieval castles of Castile. And spinally, throughout Spain, ecclesiastical history is enshrined in every community, from the small chapels and village churches of the countryside to the vertiginous towering of the great cathedrals and the mountain bulk of monasteries like Montserrat. The Moorish occupation, which so enriched Spain, leaves its traces not just in the beauties of its palaces in Granada but in the stone walls of agricultural terraces built on the higher reaches and still cultivated.

Spanish literature abounds in travelers' tales, adventures on the back roads of Spain—the early romances, the travels of Don Quixote and Sancho Panza across La Mancha, the picaresque wanderings of Lazarillo de Tormes. But all of those travels were at walking pace, or on mule back or horseback. At such a pace, to be afoot in Spain was akin to being at sea, each village a harbor, each inn an anchorage. Travelers took refuge from the landscape in these ports of human company; but so varied are these village islands that the accounts of journeys in the backlands of Spain have the dimensions of the travels of Marco Polo—a far cry from Spain now, crisscrossed by *autopistas*, with tourist highways and a web of airports; but the small villages still remain islanded, though far from unconnected now through the eye of television. Their seclusion has gone.

Those few who have written wisely and perceptibly about Spain from the outside—I think of Gerald Brenan and V.S. Pritchett in particular—speak of the experience of coming on Spain as something akin to a conversion. Many people I know, from many different cultures, have taken to Spain with the same intensity, discovering there a language, a way of life, a mode of thinking, and a diurnal rhythm somehow purifying after the complexities of their own societies. Those who settled there did so with the luxury of choice; but for the native inhabitants, their existence was a fate, a destiny, which they shouldered with an ancestral stoicism, well honed in few words, glinting with humor. Their conversations crackled with a keen sense of life and death, a dignity, an assurance. As Gerald Brenan wrote: "As they sit at their tables outside the cafes, their eyes record as on a photographic plate the people who are passing, but on a deeper level they are listening to themselves living."

I first set foot in Spain by pure chance, and found myself astonished at once at how the whole clutter of existence seemed to have been slowed down, simplified, reduced to its bony essentials but graceful in its rituals. Drawn in by it, I began to learn the language; and, after repeated visits, I went to live there. It was like growing another self, a self that thought and spoke in a different mode of being, had a wholly different history, a vast literature, a complexity of attitudes. To enter another culture, however, is not simply a matter of learning its language. I had no childhood in Spanish, so I had to educate myself, in Spanish history, in its voluminous literature, in its present writers, its press and politics, but most of all in the widely varying magnificences of its landscapes — the great solitudes of its mountains, the emptiness of great spaces relieved by the oases of small, hospitable villages. I would happily have stayed behind, for a year or two, in a dozen of them, so complete did they seem in themselves. I travelled the length and breadth of Spain, looking and listening, and I wrote a series of chronicles from Spain through the sixties and seventies for *The New Yorker* magazine. During that time, I acquired a house on the edge of a remote

One of the best preserved monuments of Roman Spain is the Aqueduct of Las Ferreras, popularly called *Puente del Diablo* (Devil's Bridge) at Tarragona. Some 217 meters across, this span of 25 arches was the vital link in a water system 35 kilometers long. Captured by the Romans in 218 B.C., Tarragona became the capital of a Roman province that stretched across Spain.

The massive round towers of La Calahorra catch the day's first light against a wintry backdrop of the Sierra Nevadas, southeast of Guadix in Andalusia.

The Casa de las Conchas in Salamanca is adorned with scallop shells identifying its owner as a Knight of Santiago, who was dedicated to protecting travelers on their pilgrimage to Compostela.

mountain village overlooking the Mediterranean, which became my headquarters for some twenty years. I entered into the ways and relationships of village life, and I saw Spain from that vantage point. The enormous changes that were taking place in the center slowed to a ripple by the time they touched our village, although touch us they did. The village had about it a long-established human rhythm, founded on agricultural abundance. It lived in an equilibrium with its own landscape that had been worked out laboriously across time. It had little will to grow, to progress, to become anything else, other than a little more comfortable. It was, as it had always been, a self-contained world.

The more I traveled in Spain, the more I saw that, off the beaten track, off the main roads between cities, off the highways that led to the new concrete tourist Meccas on the Mediterranean, lay a web of small roads that connected a whole intricate root system of villages, each with a church and a plaza at the center, and a cafe nearby where you could introduce yourself, ask questions, and find food and a bed for the night. Wherever it was, each of these villages stood in a landscape from which it drew its sustenance. To learn the particular rhythms and modes of being in one village is to make one feel at home in any of them. Yet each is unique in its private landscape, its particular climate, its crops, its terrain, its particularities, its ways.

When I first knew it, the village I settled in survived through making charcoal, the principal household fuel of those days. The men spent four days of the week in the next valley, tending the charcoal piles. The villagers made a pilgrimage to town as little as possible, to sell the charcoal, to buy supplies. Then, suddenly, like a stroke of fate, bottled gas came on the market and began to be used throughout the countryside. The charcoal trade faltered, then died. First, the men left to find work in the construction of new hotels on the coast; their wives followed, leaving the children in the care of grandparents. Houses began to close. When the children eventually left, the village school closed down, and the village was left with a skeletal population, the almonds unpicked for want of labor, the young ones leaving. Then, foreigners began to occupy the empty houses; families from the adjacent town rented them as weekend retreats; and the village took on a second life, a much more leisurely version of its former self, less isolated, less stark, with the comforts of appliances and technology, and the ubiquitousness of television. Its previous isolation had gone forever, and with it, the villagers were given choices that were never theirs till now. For them, to live in the village is no longer a fate. Yet the land continues to be cultivated, not now for the sake of survival but because, in the country, it is still the way of things.

Best known perhaps from the paintings of El Greco in the 17th century, this view of Toledo shows its strategic location at a bend in the river Tagus. One of the oldest cities in Spain, Toledo served as a capital for the Iberian tribe, the Carpetani. It was captured by the Romans in 192 B.C., regained its status as the capital of the Visigoths in A.D. 534, and was under Moorish domination from 711 until 1029 when it fell to the kings of Castile. During the Middle Ages, Toledo gained great renown as a center for scholarship and translation. The skyline of Toledo displays much of the city's history; at center is the great Gothic cathedral and at right is the fortified palace called the Alcázar, the site of numerous sieges.

And the landscapes remain. In a sense, they are human creations, for they all bear the marks of human order, the conditions and shapes of settlement and cultivation. As far as they allowed it, they have been given human design, and turned to account. They are all monuments to successive ages of human occupation, when certain proportions of people to land were arrived at, settled, and maintained. Each of these small landscapes is a map of a whole way of being, the pattern of an enduring equilibrium. While we gaze on them not without some awe from the outside, it seems important to bear in mind that, for those who lived and endured in them, each separate landscape was not just something to be looked at; it was the whole bounded world.

Alastair Reid

No better image remains of Spain's Middle Ages than castles. There are more than 2,200 scattered across the land. Not merely a castle, the Alhambra of Granada is a fortified palace-city that stretches along a spur of the Sierra Nevada mountains above the gorge of the Rio Darro. To the right are the formidable towers of the Alcazaba, the main fortress. To the left are the main rooms and courtyards of the Palace, with the Hall of the Ambassadors in the large, square tower. The Alhambra was the palace of the Moorish Nasrid kings, who founded the city in 1235 as a refuge from the Christian invaders of northern Spain. Refugees from the recently conquered Moorish kingdoms of Cordoba and Seville fled to Granada. They retained their independence until 1492, when Ferdinand and Isabel forced the city's surrender after an eight-year campaign.

Historic Spain

Crossroads of Cultures

The human presence has been felt in the Iberian peninsula since Neanderthal groups roamed the land in search of food and shelter perhaps half a million years ago. Settlements believed to be two hundred thousand years old have been found near Gibraltar, leading some scholars to suppose that these ancient peoples were only one of many waves of migration that used the peninsula as a bridge between Africa and Europe. A people known as Iberian are thought to have

arrived about nine thousand years ago. In 1100 B.C., on land jutting into the sea near Gibraltar, Phoenician sailors established what is now Cádiz, Europe's oldest continuously inhabited city. In 800 B.C. Celtic tribes moved south across the Pyrenees. Later, the Carthaginian Hannibal set up bases in Spain, and for the next two thousand years, Iberia's strategic position caused many to fight for dominion: Romans, Visigoths, Moors, French, and British invaders. Some left, but some made Spain their home and all left

Previous page: A bison painting from the caves of Altamira shows the remarkable realism of the painted caves dating from about 20,000 years ago, and located just west of Santander in Cantabria.

Spring storms boil around the towers of Segovia's Alcázar, located in Castile-Leon, a province named for its numerous castles.

Turégano, northwest of Segovia, is another impressive Castilian fortress. Founded in the 10th century, Turégano preserves only fragments of its outer wall, but a battlemented keep still shelters the Romanesque church of San Miguel.

Slender towers of the 11th-century Torre de Aragón parade across a hilltop above the town of Molina de Aragón, northeast of Guadalajara.

Castillo de Loarre perches on cliffs overlooking the plain of Aragon northwest of Huesca. A military masterpiece, the 11th-century castle was built by Sancho Ramirez, King of Navarre.

Sited high above the Guadalquivir River, Almodóvar del Rio was rebuilt in the 14th century by Pedro the First ("The Cruel") as a treasury for his spoils. Just west of Córdoba, in Andalusia, the castle is one of many that remains inhabited.

54   The huge castle of Gormaz, the longest in Europe, dominates the Duero river valley as it did in the Middle Ages when it guarded a Christian–Moorish frontier. The 10th-century castle lies southwest of Soria in Castile–Leon.

The North Coast

Galicia, Asturias, Cantabria, and the Basque Country

Thrust into the Atlantic and raked by fierce weather, Spain's northwest coast has often been referred to as the *Costa del Muerte* (Coast of Death). Moisture swept landward falls as rain on the Cantabrian mountains, making this coast the greenest area of Spain. The region farthest west, Galicia, removed from the Spanish mainstream, developed its own language and culture. Hemmed in by Portugal to the south and the kingdoms of Castile-Leon and Asturias to

the east, the Galicians, called *Gallegos* in Spanish, looked to the sea for expansion. Asturias is a rugged, mountainous land, the home of hardy miners and fishermen. Cantabria, farther east along the *Costa Esmeralda* (Emerald Coast), occupies a brilliant green strip of land squeezed between the Picos de Europa mountains and the sea. Making productive use of its heavy rainfall, Cantabria serves as Spain's dairyland. Still farther east, nestled under the Pyrenees, is Basque Country, home to a proud, independent, industrious people with a unique and ancient language.

Previous page: A gypsy girl poses against the massive doors of the great pilgrimage church at Santiago de Compostela.

Fishing boats ride peacefully at anchor in the small harbor of El Grove, just south of Cape Finisterre in Galicia.

Each July in the village of San Lorenzo de Sabucedo–La Estrada in Galicia, a rodeolike festival is held in which wild horses are brought down from the mountains to be branded and have their manes and tails cut. Called the *Rapa des Bestas*, the centuries-old practice was originally for collecting horsehair, but has become a tradition that tests the courage and strength of young men.

The 19th-century basilica of Covadonga in the rugged Cantabrian Mountains marks the site where in A.D. 718, the Visigothic nobleman, Ramon Pelayo, and a group of 300 warriors ambushed a Moorish expedition. This victory marked the beginning of the Christian reconquest of Spain from the Moors, an eight-hundred-year crusade that ended in 1492 with the fall of Granada. Nearby the basilica is Cangas de Onís, an ancient town that claims to be the first capital of Christian Spain, because it was here that Pelayo, after his victory, was crowned the first king of Asturias. *Right:* The five arches of a 13th century Romanesque bridge gracefully span the Rio Sella at Cangas de Onís. Hanging from the central arch is a replica of a Visigothic cross.

High above the villages of Covadonga and Cangas de Onís lies Lake Enol, framed by the Peña Santa Mountains. The Peña Santa massif is the northwest buttress of the Picos de Europa, not the highest mountains in Spain, but among the most severe and dramatic. Its slopes are a refuge for bears, wildcats, and chamois. *Above:* Illuminated at sunset above the valley of Valdeon, the jagged peaks of Torre Cerredo reach up to 2,648 meters, highest in the Picos de Europa.

Two villagers from Mogrevejo return from the wheat harvest; the woman at left carries her shoes because wooden clogs are worn in the fields. *Right:* An ancient farm near the village of Mogrovejo is dwarfed by the sheer walls of the Andara massif — the easternmost part of the Picos de Europa — above the valley of the Rio Deva.

Just west of Santander, near the north coast of Cantabria, the village of Santillana del Mar is considered by some to be the most beautiful village in Spain. Now a national monument, Santillana is famous for the coats of arms that decorate its medieval houses. Many of these emblems depict seafaring activities and even mermaids as the village lies only two miles from the Atlantic coast. The cloister in the village church of St. Juliana is famous for the biblical scenes depicted on its richly carved capitals.

Left: The 15th-century, Borja-Bareda Tower, center, is a gem in the necklace of mansions that surrounds the Plaza de Ramon Pelayo in Santillana del Mar.

The Pyrenees

Navarre, Aragon, La Rioja, and Catalonia

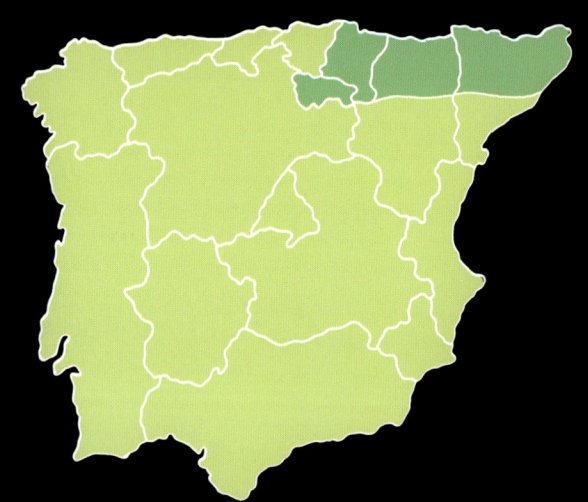

Next to Switzerland, Spain is the most mountainous country in Europe. Range after rugged range isolates many regions, sheltering villages that until modern times were all but inaccessible to the outside world. In northern Catalonia, the Valle de Arán, for example, only fifteen kilometers from the French border, was not linked by road to the rest of Spain until 1924. Not surprisingly, much Pyrenees architecture, with dormers, stepped gables, and slate roofs steeply pitched against the snows, suggests Austria rather than Spain.

At carnival time in the village of Aubert
in the Valle de Arán, children dress up in costumes.

Sited high on the valley's slope, the village of Vilamos
looks south across the Valle de Arán toward the Pico de Aneto.

Previous page: The village of Vilac, with the steep slopes of
the Valle de Arán beyond, clusters around its medieval church.

The isolated village of Pervis lies in the shadow of the Sierra de Pata,
the foothills of the Pyrenees in Catalonia.

The twin peaks of Els Encantants, soaring 2,747 meters high,
are a jewel in the National Park of Aigües Tortes in the Catalonian Pyrenees.

Near the village of Fonzaleche, autumn colors the vines of La Rioja. Although wine is produced in many parts of Spain, some of the best comes from the small northern province of La Rioja. Wine has been produced in this region since Roman times, but in the last century French vintners introduced new methods that have made these wines the equal of any in Europe.

The Mediterranean Coast

Catalonia, Valencia, and Murcia

Spain's Mediterranean Coast is actually several coastlines, each with its own character. *Costa Brava*, the "wild coast" between the French border and Barcelona, comprises a grand stretch of cliffs and beaches long thought of as the Spanish Riviera. *Costa Dorada* and *Costa del Azahar*, moving southward to Valencia, make up "the orange blossom coast" because miles of citrus groves march across the Huerta, Spain's most fertile area. Beyond lies *Costa Blanca*, the "white

coast" south of Valencia, with its glittering beach resorts. This long coastline has been

Spain's link to the Mediterranean world. From here, Hannibal sent his army against

the Roman empire. In turn, Tarragona was made the capital of Roman Spain. Later,

from Barcelona, Spanish kings launched expeditions that conquered the Balearics,

Sicily, and Naples. The importance of Spain's eastern coastline becomes apparent

when it is realized that four of the country's largest cities — Barcelona, Valencia, Murcia,

Previous page: among the many festivals of the *Costa Blanca* area that celebrate the victory of the Christians over the Moors, the one held in Villajoyosa, north of Alicante, is one of the best known.

Small bays dot the *Costa Brava*. Medieval towers and fortified walls, such as these at Tossa del Mar, are evidence of the area's strategic importance.

Sunrise illuminates the jagged pinnacles of Montserrat as they emerge from the early morning fog that wreathes its lower slopes. This mystical mountain, forty kilometers west of Barcelona, has been the spiritual heart of Catalonia since the 5th century, when hermits came here to live in isolation. Countless small chapels and hermitages remain, scattered among Montserrat's ridges and ravines. Sheltered below immense cliffs, the Benedictine monastery established here in A.D. 976 and enlarged by Philip II, has become one of Spain's most important religious centers.

An ancient street in Villafamés leads to a flight of stairs to the castle above. Above the stairs, a tiny domed roof protects a shrine to the village saint.

La Albufera, Spain's largest freshwater lagoon, lies some fifteen kilometers south of Valencia. Fishnets are staked across the narrow channel that separates La Albufera's waters from the sea.

The Interior

Castile-Leon, Castile-La Mancha, Aragon, and Estremadura

Guarded by mountain ranges on three sides, Spain's vast interior forms a high, broad plateau called the Meseta. The geography explains a climate cold in winter, sunbaked in summer, and dry because the encircling mountains wring moisture from the clouds. The Meseta was variously home to Miguel Cervantes's picaresque knight Don Quixote and the patroness of Christopher Columbus, Queen Isabel, whose culture and language—pure Castilian Spanish—

dominated the Iberian peninsula and a good part of the New World. In that regard, Estremadura, lying in the southwestern part of the plateau, was the birthplace of the Conquistadors: Cortez, the Pizarro brothers, De Soto, and Balboa all came from poor villages of the area. Many of Spain's finest castles are to be found in this land, evidence that here for centuries were the hard-fought frontiers between Christians and Moors. And in Castile-Leon are three of Spain's most beautiful cities—Segovia, Ávila, and the historic university town of Salamanca.

Previous page: A patchwork of fields. Similar patterns can be seen in many parts of the Meseta.

Vast, open space is the impression given by the Meseta. Here, windmills cluster on a ridge above fields that stretch to the horizon, southeast of Toledo.

Far from flat, the Meseta's plateau is broken by numerous mountain ranges. In the rugged Sierra del Maestrazgo, east of Teruel in Aragon, the tiny village of Linares de Mora clings to a craggy height. Located in one of the most isolated areas of the country, the town, with its ruined castle, ancient walls, and centuries-old terraced fields rises above the Rio Linares.

Following page, at left: The hanging houses of Cuenca, with their famous corbelled balconies, cling to the heights above the Jucar and Huecar rivers. This nearly impregnable site in the Sierra de Cuenca east of Madrid was variously a Roman, Visigothic, and Moorish stronghold.

Brought from the New World and more valuable in the end than the gold and silver the Conquistadors sought, was maize—seen here drying in the Aragon sun.

Rows of lavender planted on a high windy plateau stretch toward the Sierra de Albarracín, west of Teruel in Aragon.

A gateway through Albarracín's sturdy walls opens onto narrow streets and half-timbered houses.

Isolated in the rugged mountains of southern Aragon, the Moorish town of Albarracín remained an independent state long after being surrounded by Christian kingdoms.

If any city can be said to have spawned the Conquistador spirit, it is Trujillo. Five Pizarro brothers, as well as thirty-seven of their men-at-arms, left Trujillo to find fortune in the New World. *Above:* An equestrian statue of Francisco Pizarro seems to ride boldly across the *plaza mayor* in front of the cathedral. *Right:* The walls and fortified towers of Trujillo rise above the scorched landscape of Estremadura, southwest of Madrid.

In the Sierra de Guadalupe, about 100 kilometers east of Trujillo, a monastery houses a statue of the Virgin of Guadalupe, said to have been carved by St. Luke himself and rediscovered by a shepherd on this site in the 13th century. As protectress of the Conquistadors, the Virgin of Guadalupe was rewarded with gold and silver from the New World. These riches bought new chapels, bell towers, and cloisters decorated in the exotic 15th-century–Mudejar style, whose elements include horseshoe arches and the geometric patterns of Moorish Spain and North Africa. The style was created by Moorish craftsmen who lived and worked for Christian masters in reconquered areas.
Left: The first light of day illuminates Guadalupe's sumptuously decorated towers.

Following pages, at left: A hand beaten metal relief on the front door of the Monastery of Guadalupe. *At right:* A spectacular Mudejar-style rose window is framed within the horseshoe arches of the cloister of the Monastery of Guadalupe.

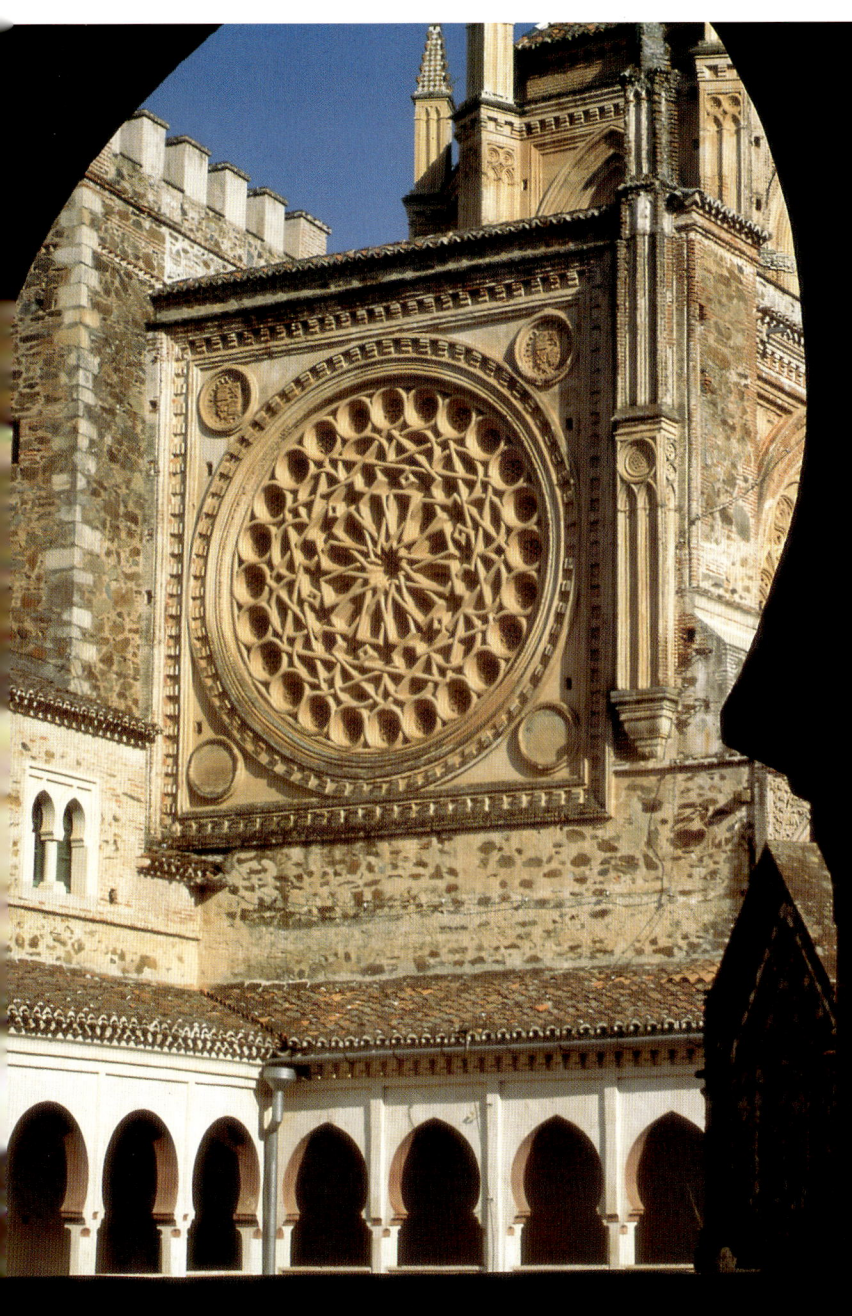

Spring storms roll across the wheat fields of Castile. *Right:* Brillant colors bring these village walls alive.

Left: A shepherd tends his flocks on the plains of Castile with the walls and towers of Segovia in the mist beyond. Dominated by its Alcázar and great 16th-century cathedral, Segovia was originally an Iberian town that became more prominent under the Romans, who strengthened the city's walls and built its famous aqueduct. During the Middle Ages it became the favorite residence of the kings of Castile and it was here, in 1474, that Queen Isabel was crowned. The Alcázar, Isabel's palace-castle, stands on a steep-sided crag between the valleys of the Erezma and the Clamores. *Right*: The cathedral and its 300-foot tower are lit by the last rays of sun. In the background, storm clouds blacken the slopes of the Guadarrama Mountains.

Children dance in a street lined with half-timbered houses.

Afternoon sun fills the *plaza mayor* of the tiny village of La Alberca, isolated in the Sierra de la Peña de Francia, south of Salamanca.

Not only the traditional architecture of wattle and plaster, but a centuries-old pattern of rural life makes villages like La Alberca national treasures. As can be seen here and on the opposite page, much social activity takes place out of doors; sitting in doorways or meeting neighbors in the intimate plazas that are the heart of each town. Such a plaza is found in Pedraza (far lower right), featuring charmingly varied columns and ancient capitals. In San Miguel de Corneja, a cart of firewood is unloaded; the docile ox wears a fringe over its eyes to keep the flies away. A barn door nearby decorated with a bull's head reflects a fascination with bulls that has persisted since the cult of Mithras in Roman times.

One of the most important religious observances in Spain is that of Corpus Christi, and nowhere is it more enthusiastically celebrated than in Toledo. For several days, processions of the faithful wind through the narrow streets, which have been covered in boughs of thyme. As if to relieve the solemnity of the occasion, parades of giant papier-mâché figures dance and whirl for the delight of younger spectators, and children wear masks of comic characters. The final procession, which begins and ends at the cathedral, includes thousands of participants, including a small group of young boys dressed in 17th-century costumes and wigs and carrying baskets of rose petals.

Andalusia

The Moorish Heartland

Andalusia, Spain's largest and most southern province, exhibits a remarkable diversity of landscapes that range from the Sierra Nevada Mountains, the peninsula's highest, to the desert arroyos of Almería. There is, in addition, an astonishing landscape that features homes cut into the rocky land itself, and Europe's largest marshland, Las Marismas, offering a unique combination of sand dunes and wetlands. The villages of Andalusia are very different from northern

villages: ancient walls, terra-cotta roofs, and hand-wrought iron balconies distinguish the *pueblos blancos*, whose whitewashed walls, tiny windows, interior courtyards, and flat roofs stacked together on mountainsides result in part because of Andalusia's sun, but perhaps even more from the strong cultural influences exerted by North Africa and other Mediterranean countries. These villages and the distinguished cities of Andalusia's provinces also mark the arrival of Spring and the coming and passing of Easter with some of Spain's most exuberant and distinctive celebrations.

Previous page: Clinging to its crag, Zahara de los Membrillos was one of many fortified Moorish villages that protected critical mountain passes surrounding the Kingdom of Granada.

A setting sun silhouettes cork trees north of Huelva in Andalusia near the Portuguese border.

Left: Near the Costa del Sol, a narrow street in Mijas is hung with pots of geraniums that provide a festive splash of red against the stark white. *Right:* A stork's nest rests undisturbed atop a bell tower in Córdoba. Considered to foster good luck and fecundity, storks are looked on with great affection by the Spanish. The birds annually migrate to winter in North Africa, often returning to the same nests in Spain and northern Europe to raise their chicks.

A large, stone cross marks one of the "Stations of the Cross" on the way to the cathedral in Montefrío, west of Granada.

Girls jump rope in Vejer de la Frontera, a mountaintop village within view of the Straits of Gibraltar.

Valued by both the Romans and Moors for its strategic position, Ronda, located east of Cádiz, sits on a high promontory cut by the Rio Guadalevin.

Arcos de la Frontera perches above a bend of the Rio Guadalete south of Seville.   127

Good Friday of Easter week in Arcos de la Frontera, as elsewhere throughout Spain, finds celebrants dressed in costumes made in colors that represent the wearers' home parishes. At far left, a father adjusts his son's cowl. At left, a statue of the Virgin is carried two miles from a parish church to the cathedral in Arcos de la Frontera. At right, on Easter Sunday in Arcos de la Frontera, a bull and up to 2,000 runners frantically hurtle along this same path in a local version of Pamplona's "Running of the Bulls."

Jerez de la Frontera in Andalusia claims two important distinctions: it is the world center for the production of fine sherry wines and the home of the elite Spanish Riding School. At left, Alvaro Domecq, president of the riding school and scion of the famous family of vintners, prepares in the school's practice ring before a performance. Below, a horse trains for the *rejoneo*, a traditional bullfight fought exclusively on horseback. At right is a *corrida* performed in the *plaza mayor* of Chinchón, southeast of Madrid. Before the introduction of bullrings in the late 18th century, all *corridas* were held this way.

The spring fairs of Andalusia last as long as four days and provide occasion for horse shows, agriculture displays, carnivals, and traditional events of all kinds. The two most famous fairs are held in Seville and Jerez de la Frontera. At left, people dance in the streets. On the opposite page, a young rider and his sister display their horsemanship before friends; a young woman is greeted by an admirer.

134   An area north of Almería near Tabernas resembles the southwestern desert of the United States so closely that it has been used for the filming of numerous Hollywood westerns. This "Mexican" town plaza still remains.

East of Granada near the town of Guadix in Andalusia is an area of tufa — porous rock laid down in deposits from springs or streams — that has become eroded and shaped into pinnacles. The tufa is easily carved and people have fashioned cavelike homes in the region for more than two thousand years. These remarkable dwellings have thick walls that provide a natural airconditioning in the tremendous heat of summer and also insulate from the cold in winter. In this unusual landscape some 6,000 persons, many of them gypsies, live in caves.
Above: Two residents of Guadix sit in the kitchen of their two-bedroom cave-home.

Plastic strips that return condensed moisture to the ground have greatly increased Andalusia's crop production.

Spring wildflowers and trees in bloom paint the rich valley of Cazorla. Located in the Sierra de Cazorla, the valley benefits from plentiful rainfall.

Ferns, poppies, and clover typify the lush Andalusian spring.
Opposite: Casares hangs precipitously on a rocky knoll in the Sierra Bermeja,
sixteen kilometers from the southern coast. Gibraltar's cliffs and Jebal Musa Mountain
on Africa's coast can be seen beyond.

The vast wetlands of the Las Marismas marsh spread toward distant islands of pine trees, resting sites for egrets and cranes on their migration route between Europe and Africa.

A vast marshland formed by the delta of the Rio Guadalquivir, Las Marismas is separated from the sea by a long ridge of sand dunes. Known officially as Doñana National Park, it is one of Europe's most important wildlife sanctuaries and houses a large indigenous population of flamingos, golden eagles, red deer, and lynx. Concern for the preservation of this habitat has increased in recent years due to rice farming on the adjacent lands and the development of resorts along the coast. In addition to its feathered and furred residents, Las Marismas annually plays host to thousands of pilgrims during Pentecost. Processions of gaily decorated, ox-drawn carts converge from all directions on the tiny town of El Rocío in the heart of Las Marismas. Above, pilgrims break camp at sunrise and prepare their donkeys for another day of travel.

Umbrella pines rise above sand dunes in Doñana National Park.

Flocks of flamingos live in the Las Marismas marshlands.

A group dressed in flamenco skirts and caballero outfits breaks for song and dance on the dunes above the sea.

The pilgrimage of El Rocío occurs every year at Pentecost, the seventh Sunday after Easter. Thousands of participants travel on horseback, by cart, or on foot to pay homage to the shrine of the "Virgin of the Dew," Nuestra Señora del Rocío. Above léft, a line of carts crosses the dunes of Doñana. At lower left, an ox cart fords a stream northeast of El Rocío. They may travel as much as five days to reach their goal, a shrine housing a wooden statue said to date from the time the Visigoths introduced Christianity to Spain. For pilgrims to El Rocío, the statue is a symbol of miracles past and present, not the least of which was its reappearance in the 12th century after having been hidden for five hundred years during the Moorish occupation.

On Pentecost, at two o'clock in the morning, the revered statue of the Virgin is carried into the streets of the village. Thousands of pilgrims vie for the right to bear the holy effigy as children and women are passed over the heads of those along the route to touch the hem of the Virgin's cloak. Priests are borne on the shoulders of their parishioners and beseech the Virgin for blessings. As many as 500,000 persons may be present and so packed are the streets of El Rocío that it may take sixteen hours for the statue to make its way through the town and back to its sanctuary.
Above: Upon reaching El Rocío a father and his son light candles in a chapel of the shrine.
Left: A young shepherd looks on and a giant Osborne bull seems to survey the activity.

154   At Cerro Gordo, near Almuñécar east of Málaga, the mountainous coastline of Andalusia meets the sea. An ancient watchtower silhouetted on its rocky promontory still guards against an attack of Barbary pirates.

The Balearic and Canary Islands

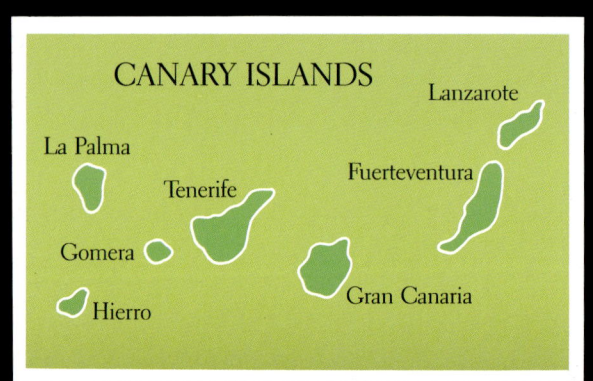

Once the dominant seafaring nation, Spain has long valued its islands. The Balearics mainly comprise: Minorca, Ibiza, Formentera, and Majorca, the largest. The Canary Islands, lying sixty miles off southern Morocco, are tropical. All seven major islands are volcanic, containing spectacular landscapes. Tenerife has Spain's highest peak; Lanzarote features Timanfaya National Park; and Gomera, one of the smallest main islands, boasts Garajonay National Park, created in a volcanic crater to preserve the world's largest laurel rainforest.

Previous page: The coastal plains near Palma de Mallorca are dotted with delicate, stone windmills that draw water for this fertile region.

The harbor of Palma de Mallorca, capital of the Balearics, is visible as a ray of light breaks through storm clouds and illuminates the great Gothic cathedral and the walls of the old city.

Wildflowers bloom below the jagged silhouettes of Los Roques, part of a twisted and eroded volcanic ridge in the Cañadas plateau on Tenerife.

These rocks, near Pico de Teide on Tenerife, have been shaped into exotic forms by the action of wind and water.

A view toward Timanfaya volcano shows the lunar landscape of Timanfaya National Park, also called *Las Montañas del Fuego* (The Mountains of Fire) on Lanzarote.

Rich vineyards in the La Geria valley on Lanzarote are planted on volcanic slopes, in pits dug through the layers of ash and surrounded with stone walls as windbreaks to protect the young vines.

El Golfo, on the southwest coast of Lanzarote, is an extinct volcanic crater now eroded and open to the sea, its walls sheltering a lagoon.

On La Gomera island a picturesque church near the village of La Calera seems nearly overwhelmed with tropical vegetation in the steep-sided *Valle Gran Rey* (Valley of the Great King).

The mountainous terrain of La Gomera captures moisture from the trade winds, giving birth to a lush rainforest in what is now Garajonay National Park. The laurel trees, a relic form, survive from the days before the Ice Age.

A note from the photographer

I visited Spain for the first time in 1966. My first impressions, and they remain vividly with me, were of vast, open spaces. The landscape had a scale to it that I had not experienced in other European countries. I also felt instantly at home in Spain, possibly because at least some of the magnificent country I saw reminded me of the southwestern United States, and also because the ancient villages, terraced fields, and castles that I saw conveyed a sense of history, of long human habitation. These strong first impressions have drawn me back more than twenty times since my first visit. As many miles as I have traveled in Spain, each trip has brought revelations — an isolated, unexplored valley, new vistas, colors, and textures. But, above all, I have enjoyed wonderful encounters and special moments with the people of rural Spain: walking with a shepherd in a drenching spring rain as Segovia's remarkable silhouette rose through the mist in the background; helping two grandmothers harvest their wheat in a Cantabrian meadow; entering an ancient cave home in Andalusia where a husband and wife posed proudly at their kitchen table; and traveling the dusty trails of Doñana in the heartwarming comradery of the El Rocío pilgrimage. Such memories are the best thing that Spain can offer.

Acknowledgments

M y work on this book would not have been possible without the generous support of many people in the United States and in Spain. In particular, I would like to thank my good friend Mario Trinidad, Midwest Director of the Spanish Tourist Office, and his staff, especially Patricia Wood, for their endless patience and assistance; Victoria Ayuso of the Tourist Office of Spain in New York for her insight and encouragement from the beginning of this project; Germán Porras, Miguel Ortega, and Julián Abad of Turespaña in Madrid for their support and guidance; David González, General Manager of Iberia Airlines-Midwest USA, and his staff for enthusiasm and encouragement; the managers and staff of numerous Spanish Paradors for their warm hospitality; and Juan Carlos Orlando of I.T.E.L./Madrid. For their enduring patience and helpful advice, I wish to thank Midge Keator, Woodfin Camp, and Tennyson Schad. At Abrams, I would like to express my appreciation to Robert Morton for his guidance and perceptive editing, to Liz Trovato for her imaginative design, and to Alastair Reid for his sensitive opening essay. In addition, I must express a special appreciation to those close friends who encouraged and supported my efforts: Walter and Sara Van Enck, Charles Seaborn, Paco Lopez of Comtours, and Katherine. Thanks also to my staff at Odyssey Productions for the hard work that allowed me the time to carry through this project.

For my photographic work, I used a Fuji G617 camera and Fuji 50 film for the panoramas that I felt were necessary to capture the scale of the land. Additionally, I used Nikon 35mm cameras and lenses and a mix of Fuji 50 and Kodachrome film for photographing festivals and people.

Above all, I owe the realization of this book to my friends and assistants Lani Barton, Hillary Lamphear, and Kevin Martin, who walked many miles, rose for many sunrises, and waited patiently with me those long hours for that special light.

Finally, I dedicate this book to my father.